Journey through

STUTTGART

Photos by
Tina und Horst Herzig

Text by
Michael Kühler

Stürtz

8

Page 10/11:
Stuttgart's museum of natural history moved to Schloss Rosenstein in 1954. The neoclassical palace was built by Giovanni Salucci (1769–1845) at the instigation of King Wilhelm I between 1822 and 1830.

Contents

12

Swabian *dolce vita* on the Neckar and Nesenbach

26

From the main station to the Wilhelmsbau – the centre
Page 46
The (hi)story of Württemberg's ducal and royal seat
Page 68
Modern and post-modern architecture – mecca on the Neckar

80

North, south, east and west – the inner districts
Page 94
Bubbles on your skin – Stuttgart's mineral water

110

From Bad Cannstatt to Wangen – the suburbs
Page 124
A city of and for cars – Mercedes-Benz and Porsche

134 Index
135 Map
136 Credits

Page 28/29:
Schlossplatz, with its
jubilee column, fountains
and old chancellery with
the gilt statue of Mercury.
In the background are the
two very different spires of
the collegiate church.

The chapel in the Altes
Schloss or old palace was
consecrated in 1562. The
Renaissance ceiling dates
back to the 16th century,
with the rest of the décor
the result of neo-Gothic
refurbishment in 1865.

This archway leads out
from the courtyard of the
Altes Schloss onto Schillerplatz. Here, the Alte
Kanzlei or old chancellery
houses a restaurant of the
same name (right) and the
Prinzenbau in the
background a ministry.

Right page:
The inner quadrant of the
Altes Schloss is heralded
as one of the most
beautiful Renaissance
courtyards in Germany.
Until the mid 18th century
the palace was the seat of
the counts and later dukes
of Württemberg. It's now
Württemberg's regional
museum (Landesmuseum).

Page 32/33:
The pavement cafés in the Königsbau have extended their 'territory' out to the edge of the grass on Schlossplatz. Here, with a glass of something refreshing in front of you, you can sit and observe the passers-by on Königstrasse and those admiring the jubilee column.

Left page:
The arcade in the Königsbau is the oldest of its kind in Stuttgart. Here it's usually much quieter than on Königstrasse, with plenty of specialist shops to peruse at your leisure.

Left:
The vast Königsbau-Passagen mall, packed with shops and other business premises, has been built onto the façade of the Königsbau. The lofty foyer is a fine place to savour some German Kaffee und Kuchen or coffee and cake.

The art museum café has become one of the most popular places in town – not least for its splendid location. If you've manage to secure one of the much-sought-after seats on the terrace, you can sit back and enjoy the colourful urban scene before you, often enlivened by various street performers.

The building to the right of the Königsbau was once Hotel Marquardt and is still one of the most distinctive edifices on Schlossplatz. The square marks the invisible boundary between Obere and Untere Königstrasse, the longest and most popular street of shops in Stuttgart.

Lion standing guard on the court of honour at the Neues Schloss or new palace. His shield depicts the coat of arms of the kingdom of Württemberg, with three lions representing the Staufer dynasty and three sets of antlers for Württemberg.

Right page:
Through the glass façade of the art museum you can gaze out over Schlossplatz to the Kunstgebäude or art building and part of the Neues Schloss, with Stuttgart's famous heights in the background. On the left are the columns adorning the Königsbau.

Right:
The glass façade of the art museum has performed a minor urban miracle in that it now greatly enhances the appearance of Kleiner Schlossplatz which has been a bone of contention since it was laid out in 1969.

Far right:
The restaurant on the top floor of the art museum is aptly named Cube. The café/bar in the basement has the arty title of no title: o.T. or „ohne Titel".

Right:
At the art museum exhibitions are advertised by enormous letters stuck onto the glass façade which cast their shadow in the interior. The very word „Art" is thus an art it itself ...

Far right:
The bar in o.T. is extremely minimalist in design, calling for the various bottles to be kept in very tidy order. The café acts as a perfect interface between the mad bustle outside on the streets and the ethereal clam of the museum – a fine place to prepare yourself for the delights that await on either side of the divide.

Above:
The main building of the state theatre is situated on the Eckensee, an extremely shallow expanse of water interspersed with energetic fountains. The theatre rose to fame in the second half of the 20th century through its ballet, directed by South African choreographer John Cranko (1927–1973).

Right:
The state theatre in Stuttgart performs not just drama and comedy but also ballet and opera. This fountain is known as the Fountain of Fate, built in 1914 in memory of opera diva Anna Sutter who was murdered by a jilted lover.

Left:
Next to the Grosses Haus of the state theatre the regional government of Baden-Württemberg has its parliament building, erected at the beginning of the 1960s. Its sober, quadratic, dark brown design forms a stark contrast to the more halcyon setting of Oberer Schlossgarten.

Below:
The park of Oberer Schlossgarten is an open-air living room in the centre of town. Many come here to relax and maybe read a good book or two.

Left:
Café Nil is a big attraction in Mittlerer Schlossgarten. Its terrace, built into the lake, provides an oasis of calm nearly all year round.

Below:
The plans for the contro-versial Stuttgart 21 station project envisaged about 300 trees being felled in Mittlerer Schlossgarten. Mediator Heiner Geissler demanded that they be replanted elsewhere, a practically impossible task with trees that are in part up to 200 years old ...

Page 44/45:
The choir of the Stiftskirche or collegiate church on Schillerplatz is festooned with remarkable epitaphs to the counts and dukes of Württemberg. The Renais-sance façade of Frucht-kasten, the old granary, on the right was designed by Württemberg's master builder Heinrich Schickhardt (1558–1635).

THE (HI)STORY OF WÜRTTEMBERG'S DUCAL AND ROYAL SEAT

In 2029 the city of Stuttgart can celebrate the 800th anniversary of its first official mention. What is now the suburb of Bad Cannstatt is much older as it was once a Roman settlement. However, it can be safely said that Stuttgart is rightly the state capital of Baden-Württemberg as it fell to the House of Württemberg as part of a dowry from a Baden margravine. Its further development was decisively shaped by the fact that the city – with a few interruptions – was the seat of the counts, dukes and later kings of Württemberg.

Once upon a time the regional capital was nearly Bad Urach; following the Treaty of Münsingen in 1482, however, which reunited a county divided, Count Eberhard the Bearded kept Stuttgart on as his traditional place of residence. He was made the first duke of Württemberg in 1495, commemorated by a statue of him on horseback in the courtyard of the Altes Schloss. A few decades later, in 1534, Duke Ulrich sanctioned the Reformation. Thanks to this auspicious event, to this very day there are a few days missing from Stuttgart's history books. The Protestants introduced the Gregorian Calendar decreed by the pope in 1582 much later than the Catholics, with the result that in the year 1700 February 18 was immediately followed by March 1.

Unlike most medieval castles the Altes Schloss in Stuttgart was not built on a hill but as a moated castle in a valley, this made feasible by its remote location. It's very probable that the Stutengarten (literally „stud garden") which gave Stuttgart its name was once on what is now Schillerplatz. The ruler with the greatest enthusiasm for building was undoubtedly Duke Carl Eugen who ruled both the city and the country from 1744 to 1793. A generous donation by the citizens of Stuttgart finally persuaded him to move his ducal seat from the comfortable palace in Ludwigsburg back to Stuttgart – and to cement his return he had the Neues Schloss erected. He was also responsible for the palaces of Solitude and Hohenheim.

The first orangery in Germany was the Altes Lusthaus. Its successor the Neues Lusthaus, the ruins of which stand in the central palace gardens, has only managed to survive at all thanks to a local action group – and, again, hefty donations. This tradition of public pride and interest may not always have been agreeable to those in power but nevertheless it was this which in the mid 20th century saved the Neues Schloss from total annihilation. If a dedicated section of the local population have their way, in a similar vein the station and Hotel Silber, once a Gestapo headquarters, will also be spared the demolition teams.

Lord, give us brains!

Herr, schmeiß Hirn ra! or Lord, Give Us Brains! is the title of a book by local author Gerhard Raff, published in 1985, which has become something of a local saying in Stuttgart. In 1995 the sequel *Mehr Hirn!* (More Brains!) was issued, illustrated by famous German comedian Loriot. Raff's plea to the Almighty is justified when we learn just how many historical buildings have been unnecessarily torn down since the Second World War. There are many legacies of the former kingdom of Württemberg still standing, however: the Königsbau and Kunstgebäude or art building on Schlossplatz, Wilhelmspalais, Schloss Rosenstein and Schloss Wilhelma in Cannstatt – and last but not least the chapel of rest on the Württemberg. Not only Stuttgart's kings – by the grace of Napoleon – were active; their wives also did their fair share of charitable and cultural works for the city. This is impressively described by Sabine Thomsen, niece of historian Hansmartin Decker-Hauff, in her book *Die württembergischen Königinnen* or The Queens of Württemberg.

Stuttgart was also where the first Socialist congress in Germany took place, with Rosa Luxemburg as main speaker and Carla Zetkin as Lenin's 'host'. The world's first Waldorf or Steiner school was founded in Stuttgart, with the first university of agriculture established at Hohenheim. The main station by Bonatz took 14 years to build due to the deprivations of the First World War and the ensuing hyperinflation; it will take just as long (2014) until Stuttgart finally again has a museum of city history after the previous establishment of this kind was closed down in the Tagblatt Tower. Until then, the stories and histories of the Swabian metropolis can be perused at leisure in Harald Schukraft's epistle entitled *Wie Stuttgart wurde, was es ist* or How Stuttgart Came To Be What It Is Today.

Left:
Wilhelm II, the fourth and last king of Württemberg, is remembered by a statue of him and his dogs outside the Wilhelmspalais, erected in 1991.

Above:
Huge blocks of stone on Karlsplatz, shown against the backdrop of the Altes Schloss, commemorate the victims of National Socialism.

Small photos, right, from top to bottom: King Wilhelm I had a chapel of rest built for his second wife, Katharina Pavlovna from St Petersburg, on the top of Württemberg Hill.

This statue in the courtyard of the Altes Schloss is of Eberhard the Bearded (1445–1496), the man made the first duke of Württemberg in 1495.

The Neues Schloss was badly damaged during the Second World War. Not long afterwards there were plans afoot to tear it down and replace it with a new department store; this was prevented by hefty protest from the local population.

These glass panels suspended from the roof of the Stiftskirche are not designed to detract from the historic fabric of the collegiate church but to improve the acoustics for the many concerts held here.

The Stiftskirche is the chief Protestant church in Württemberg. Its interior was extensively restored in 2000 and is once again one of the Stuttgart's local architectural treasures.

In 1839 Danish sculptor Bertel Thorvaldsen (1770–1844) created Germany's first monument to Schiller which stands on Schiller-platz outside the Altes Schloss. The fairytale „The Old Church Bell" by his fellow countryman Hans Christian Andersen (1805–1875) is about how the statue was made.

The place where local reg-isters, ledgers and stores were once kept is now occupied by the traditional Alte Kanzlei restaurant. The establishment in the old chancellery has two terraces, one in the shade and one in the sun here on Schillerplatz.

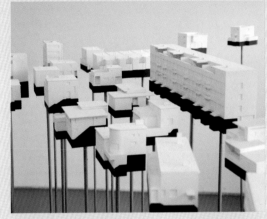

Small photos, right, from top to bottom:
In the space of just 21 weeks 21 houses containing 63 apartments were put up at the Weissenhofsiedlung. This house was planned by architect Peter Behrens (1868–1940).

In a semi-detached house designed by Le Corbusier (1887–1965) and Pierre Jeanneret (1896–1967) in the Weissenhofsiedlung a museum devoted to the same was opened in 2006. It contains a model of the famous estate.

The spectacular new Porsche Museum designed by the Viennese Delugan Meissl architectural bureau was opened in 1009.

Like the state gallery, the main building of the music conservatoire is by British architect James Stirling, completed after his death by his colleague Michael Wilford.

Below:
The Grand Café Planie has been ensconced in Stuttgart's old orphanage for several years now. Minsters from the neighbouring local authorities can often be found rubbing shoulders with locals and tourists at its wickerwork tables and chairs, which are especially well frequented when there's a flea market on.

Top right:
Sculptor Josef Zeiler was responsible for much of the plastic artwork on the houses on Geissplatz as well as its fountain. The area was torn down and rebuilt in the local style from 1906 onwards and is now considered one of the prettiest spots in the city centre.

Centre right:
This statue on horseback in the middle of Karlsplatz is of Kaiser Wilhelm I. The square was once the duchess' garden which was levelled between 1775

and 1778 after the official Württemberg residence had been moved back from Ludwigsburg to Stuttgart. The street between the two palaces is thus now known locally as Planie or the plain.

Bottom right:
This angel and lute adorn the base of Schiller's statue on Schillerplatz outside the Altes Schloss. The square not only provides an attractive backdrop for the weekly market; it's also the venue of the wine festival and Christmas market, bringing added life and colour to the middle of the city.

Strictly speaking, the
television tower has 'only'
been a radio tower since
2006, with radio pro-
grammes now broadcast
from it. The edifice was
designed by Stuttgart
engineer Fritz Leonhardt
(1909–1999).

Above:
This panoramic view stretches from Karlshöhe in the west, across the district of Stuttgart-West and the inner city to the other side of the River Neckar and Bad Cannstatt. On the horizon, in the north, the Württemberg Unterland begins.

Right:
Up here you have the entire centre of Stuttgart at your feet. From the Rathaus (left) to Schloss-garten and the main station you can see out as far as Burgholzhof (in the background on the right), surrounded by vineyards.

Right:
Like many others, the Bismarck Tower in Stuttgart was built to a prize-winning design by architect Wilhelm Kreis (1873–1955), entitled „The Twilight of the Gods". The tower is on Gähkopf in the north of the city and had grand views out in all directions.

Below:
There are pleasant views of Stuttgart-West to be had from the Bismarck Tower. Karlshöhe is to the left on the horizon and to the right is the Hasenberg, with the forest of Degerloch beyond.

Above:
Like in many other German cities Stuttgart also has its mountain of rubble where the remains of the buildings bombed in the Second World War are stored. In the 1950s Birkenkopf Hill grew an additional 40 metres or 130 feet due to the amount of debris stored here.

Left:
The rich embellishments that once adorned Stuttgart's houses can be found in the Lapidarium park on Mörikestrasse and of course here on Birkenkopf Hill or Monte Scherbelino (Mount Rubble), as it's known locally.

Left:
The Johanneskirche with its idyllic lake-side setting, once outside the city gates, is now part of Stuttgart-West. After being damaged during the Second World War the steeple was rebuilt without its helm roof, with the church now acting as a memorial to the horrors of war.

Below:
View up the spiral staircase of the beautiful neo-Gothic interior of the Johanneskirche.

Below:
There are many fine examples of wrought ironwork inside the Johanneskirche.

Bottom:
For a Protestant church the Johanneskirche is incredibly decorative. It's heralded as a masterpiece of the neo-Gothic, built between 1864 and 1876 by head architect Christian Friedrich von Leins (1814–1892) who was also responsible for Villa Berg, the Königsbau and the pavilion on Schlossplatz.

One of the most splendid fountains in Stuttgart is the Galatea Brunnen on Eugensplatz. Its creation was commissioned by Queen Olga from St Peterberg in an attempt to make the city more beautiful. On its unveiling some citizens of Stuttgart loudly voiced their disgust that the figure of Galatea atop the fountain was too sparsely clad. Queen Olga was not amused and hotly retorted that perhaps she should turn the statue round so that it presented its backside to the city ...

Right page:
Stuttgart is famous for its many flights of steps. Those open to the public, such as the Eugenstaffel depicted here, enable quick and easy access from the heights to the valley floor. Going back up takes a little longer ...

Left:
The Chinese Garden first
went on show in Rosen-
stein Park for the IGA
international gardening
exhibition held in 1993.
As it attracted so many
visitors, after the show
had finished it was moved
to a site on the corner of
Birkenwaldstrasse and
Panoramastrasse.

Below:
The Chinese Garden is
maintained by a society
founded to make Stuttgart
more beautiful which
celebrated its 150th anniversary in 2011.

Left:
Simple, sharp lines
abound at the Weissenhof-
siedlung. The different
colour of the houses
prevents the estate from
being too monotonous in
its design.

Centre left:
As opposed to many
housing estates being
built today, at the
Weissenhofsiedlung the
stringent architectural
forms were broken by
deliberately rounded
corners.

Bottom left:
In one half of the Weissenhof Museum various
exhibits are on display;
the second half consists
of a house kept in the style

of the day. The Weissen-
hofsiedlung was part of
an exhibition initiated in
1927 by the Deutscher
Werkbund entitled „Die
Wohnung" (The House).

Left:
The Weissenhof Museum
was set up in this semi-
detached house in 2006
after the building had
been restored to its origi-
nal state. The museum
features many historic
documents and
architectural models.

Right:
In the Heusteigviertel on the corner of Filderstrasse and Römerstrasse stands one of Germany's most unusual churches. The Markuskirche is an orgy of Jugendstil, as this portal richly illustrates.

Far right:
The steeple of the Markuskirche was one of the first worldwide to be built in reinforced concrete. As the concrete is plastered over, the building looks much older.

Right:
The interior of the Markuskirche spans the transition from Historicism to Jugendstil. Neo-Romanesque pillars and a Renaissance barrel vaulting form a stark contrast to the turn-of-the-century ornamentation of 1906.

Right page:
Stuttgart is the only state capital in Germany with its own expanses of vineyard. Some are owned by the city; others are managed by private winegrowers, known locally as „Wengerter", or cooperatives.

Above:
Angels are usually found in abundance in cemeteries and the Pragfriedhof is no exception. It's the third largest in town and when it was first laid out in 1873 it lay beyond the city boundaries.

Right and far right:
Many famous people have found their final resting place in the Pragfriedhof. They include famous Swabian writer Eduard Mörike (1804–1875), publisher Alfred Kröner (1861–1922), aviation pioneer Ferdinand Graf von Zeppelin (1838–1917) and various members of the Marquardt hotelier family.

Above:
The Jugendstil crematorium in the Pragfriedhof is the only one of its kind in Stuttgart. It also has a columbarium where urns are installed. Cabaret artist and singer Claire Waldoff (1884–1957) is laid to rest here.

Left:
This practically naked male angel adorning a grave in Stuttgart's Pragfriedhof is rare, with most of his funereal counterparts both female and less scantily clad.

Right:
Perhaps Stuttgart's most unusual 'cemetery' is the Lapidarium on Mörike-strasse. This small, enchanting park contains the remains of old houses and masonry from graves and buildings that have long since disappeared.

Below:
Rosenstein Park in Bad Cannstatt is the largest informally landscaped park in the southwest of Germany. Just outside the palace is a decidedly more formal rose garden, its symmetrical beds nevertheless just as inviting and pleasing to the senses.

Above:
The old palace of Schloss Rosenstein now houses a museum of natural history. When the palace was built for King Wilhelm I of Württemberg the monarch stressed that he should have an unhindered view of the chapel of rest on Württemberg Hill.

Left:
Outside the palace is a copy of the group of nymphs by sculptor Johann Heinrich Dannecker (1758–1841). As hunting is prohibited in Rosenstein Park it has the densest population of rabbits in Germany, with about 100 animals per 100 hectares or ca. 250 acres of land.

Above:
When a mineral spring was discovered on the site of what is now the Wilhelma, King Wilhelm I decided to have a bathing house erected here. The result was an oriental palace, complete with vast filigree glasshouses.

Right:
The botanical gardens at the Wilhelma include a tropical jungle with a cool waterfall.

Far right:
One of the most popular places at the Wilhelma is the elephant compound. The oldest cow elephant in Europe once lived here; born in 1949, Vilja died of a circulatory collapse in 2010.

Above:
Another of the highlights at the Wilhelma zoological gardens is the water lily pond. Several times a week the pond gardener wades into the heated water to remove faded blooms or collect seed for the following season.

Far left:
Polar bear Wilbär, born in the Wilhelma in 2007, is more fortunate than his 'cousins' Knut in Berlin Zoo and Flocke in Nuremberg who were both rejected by their mothers.

Left:
Succulents, palms, ferns and many other Mediterranean, tropical and subtropical plants all feel perfectly at home in the glasshouses of the Wilhelma.

109

From Bad Cannstatt to Wangen – the suburbs

The most famous vineyards in Stuttgart are those between the villages of Rotenberg and Uhlbach. They are a pleasant and popular place to walk whatever the time of year.

It was at the beginning of the 20th century that Stuttgart grew to its present size, with what were small villages and satellite towns being officially swallowed up by the metropolis. One of these was Cannstatt which became a *Bad* or spa in the 1930s. The people of Cannstatt still consider themselves to be *Cannstätter* and not *Stuttgarter* – which is hardly surprising as the vast suburb on the far side of the River Neckar has a lot to offer: a snug, fully intact old town centre, the impressive Wilhelma palace and gardens and the popular Wasen festival, second only to Munich's Oktoberfest.

Next door, also in the Neckar valley, are Obertürkheim and Untertürkheim. This is the home of Daimler and also wine, which can also be found aplenty in Uhlbach and Rotenberg, beneath and on the Württemberg. It was on this hill, which once leant its name to an entire country, that King Wilhelm I had a chapel of rest built for his second wife Katharina Pavlovna from St Petersburg. The former royal palace of Rosenstein is now a museum of natural history; Schloss Hohenheim, a country seat which Duke Carl Eugen erected for his mistress and later wife Franziska, now accommodates a university of the same name.

Many of Stuttgart's sights can be found on the outskirts, such as the Veitskirche in Mühlhausen, Degerloch with its television tower and the pretty centres of Wangen and Hofen, the last a Catholic enclave in the middle of Protestant Württemberg. Architectural and industrial highlights are on show at the Mercedes-Benz and Porsche museums. The historic division of land more or less forced many Swabians to become do-it-yourself enthusiasts to survive; their great skill in doing so is embodied in the invention and development of the automobile.

Below:
Duke Carl Eugen once had himself a summer residence built in Rotwildpark, naming it Bärenschlössle or bear palace not after the animal but after a local stream. King Wilhelm I later had a hunting lodge erected on the same site, the 1990s reconstruction of which is now a favourite country inn.

Top right:
Dead wood mirrored in the Bärensee. The beautiful, unadulterated scenery of the grounds enclosing the Bärenschlössle makes it very popular with walkers, joggers, hikers and cyclists.

Centre right:
In 1964 Lilli Kerzinger-Werth (1897–1971) fashioned the two bronze bears outside the Bären-schlössle after originals

Below:
King Wilhelm I had the famous chapel of rest on top of Württemberg Hill built for his second wife Katharina Pavlovna from the House of Romanov-Holstein-Gottorp (1788–1819). She died young: people say it was due to her husband's infidelity but the real cause was a hyperinfection of the head.

Right:
Above the entrance to the chapel on Württemberg Hill King Wilhelm I had the following words inscribed: „Love never stops". The mausoleum was inspired by Andrea Palladio's Villa Rotunda near Vicenza in Veneto and was built by Florentine architect Giovanni Salucci.

Right page:
The hills that surround the village of Rotenberg are the foothills of the Schurwald that in turn are enclosed by the Stuttgart suburbs of Untertürkheim and Uhlbach and the town of Fellbach. A good two percent of Stuttgart is covered in vineyards, most of which are fairly steep, as the photo illustrates.

Right:
The Ochsen or ox in Uhlbach has long been a popular country pub. The wine tavern even has its own rather rude song dedicated to it, sung to a famous hymn tune. As to be expected, it serves good, hearty Swabian fare, including roast with plenty of onions and Maultaschen or Swabian ravioli. Potato salad is made with stock; the Swabians like their food 'wet', i.e. with lots of sauce. Specialities such as pork jowl are served with Spätzle, the Swabian version of Italian pasta. The jury is still out as to which variation came first …

Page 132/133:
From Württemberg Hill there are grand views of the sun-kissed village of Uhlbach. Wine is cultivated and drunk here and there is even a wine museum packed with information on the history of and anecdotes told about Stuttgart's local alcoholic beverages which include Trollinger, Cannstatter Zuckerle and Schillerwein.